How To Do Magic That Works

The Ultimate Technique for Making
Things Happen

Genevieve Davis

Contents

Chapter One

HOW TO DO MAGIC THAT WORKS

Let me show you how to do magic that *works*.

I'm going to teach you a simple, magical way to change your day-to-day experience of the world. A way to affect your life for the better, moment by moment. A way to get things to *go your way*. A ridiculously simple way to *make things happen*.

I call it 'The Ultimate Technique'.

Are you looking for better finances, great relationships, resolution of old problems, luck and good fortune, fun, adventure or just a generally happier experience of life? There is no reason why these good things cannot be yours. All that is needed is a little effort to nudge things in the direction you want them to go. This is where *The Ultimate Technique* come in. It is the easiest and most effective way I know to shift direction, get the magic working and cause massive changes as a result.

This is the sixth book I've written on the subject of using magic to create a better life. But this magic is not witchcraft. It does not involve energies or candles or raising spirits. It is simply a way of doing things a little differently. And in a way that leads to an exceptionally fun and effortless life.

I've been working with magic for over ten years and I like to think I've become pretty good at it. But just occasionally, a flash of insight will still come along and stop me in my tracks. I'll slap my forehead and wonder, 'Why didn't I think of that before?'

The Ultimate Technique is the result of one of those insights.

There is a sense of 'obviousness' about *The Ultimate Technique.* You may find yourself thinking, 'Of course it works this way!' or even wondering why you didn't think of it yourself. The technique can be learnt quickly and started instantly. You could begin using it before you've even finished reading the book.

This is an advanced technique, but in many ways, it's just an extension of what I have taught before. It is a direct development of my 'Magic Words' technique from my book, *Magic Words and How to Use Them*. Those familiar with my work should find it easy. But even those new to my work should be able to get the hang of it. Anyone can do it, and results tend to come rapidly.

But why the 'ultimate' technique?

At some point on this spiritual path, often only after we've created all that we could ever want, we get to the stage of no longer needing to change the outside world.

We start to realise we *never* needed to change the outside world. At this point, the need for techniques, tools and methods for *making things better* drops away.

So there's a lot more to this short book than a manifestation technique for changing our physical world. There are also tantalising glimpses of what lies beneath this physical world, to what's *really* here, what's *really* true.

This is where the Law of Attraction meets non-duality. At the juncture of this place, I offer this, my ultimate technique for *making things happen*. I hope you love it as much as I do.

Chapter Two

WHY ARE YOU HERE?

Why do we start the spiritual journey? Why do we begin looking towards self-help, or spirituality or 'another way' of doing things? For me, it was simple.

Suffering.

Ten years ago, my life was in the pits. I was in debt, I was hopeless, I was lonely, and I was chronically depressed. When at my lowest point, I took my first step on this long, astonishing spiritual journey. For one reason—to fix my broken life. I wanted bigger, I wanted more, I wanted things and circumstances that I believed would make everything better.

At the time, it seemed obvious to me that the only way to improve my experience of life would be to improve my external circumstances. I needed money, a different job, a better home, friends, and a nice partner—all things I didn't have. And because I didn't have them, I deduced that simply having these missing things would complete my life and make me happy. Unsurprisingly, in those early days, my focus was entirely on getting stuff, changing stuff and making stuff happen. I needed control, so I thought. I needed power over my life and the events that took place in it. And so I threw myself into studying, and mastering the art of 'manifestation'.

Like a lot of people, I began this journey by reading books. My early reading included *The Secret* by Rhonda Byrne, *Think and Grow Rich* by Napoleon Hill and other books on the law of attraction.

A few years later, I'd become pretty good with manifestation, and my life was unrecognisable. I now had the money, the house, the car, the friends, and the man. My first books on magic were even subtitled *A course in manifesting an exceptional life*, because that's what I appeared to have done. I really did seem to have manifested an exceptional life using magic.

As time has passed, my understanding has deepened. I've come to the same conclusion as so many others before me: the true source of happiness is not in things or stuff. I've come to see that the desire to manifest or create particular things is nothing more than a misunderstanding of how experience and reality work. And as this realisation has deepened, my obsession with obtaining things and creating the right circumstances has gradually ebbed away.

And, as a result, something strange and fascinating has happened.

As my insistence on getting things right has lessened, things have only got 'better'. By not being concerned with 'the way everything turns out', my life has become more effortless, more peaceful, and more fun. I also have considerably less fear, and I experience a lot less suffering.

As I've stopped trying to force the material world to be a certain way, the material world has improved. I've stopped wanting more money, and have simply become richer. I've stopped needing my businesses to be successful and they've become ridiculously so. I've stopped being desperate to find friends and my social life has become perfect. In other words, I've 'manifested more stuff'. And the really interesting part is that these material results have not come about because I have consciously tried to make things happen, but largely because *I have stopped trying to do so.*

As it turns out, our striving to change the world, our demands that it be a certain way are not a route to happiness, but what stands in the way of it. Most bizarrely, we receive more of what we want by *not* requiring the world to be a certain way.

The technique I offer in this book comes directly from a workshop I held in 2022 as part of my membership program, *The Academy of Magic.* However, I have made a great effort to make this book totally worthwhile and effective in its own right, even without the full Academy teachings. You should be able to go away from this book with a perfect working understanding of how to make *The Ultimate Technique* work for you.

At the end of this book, I'm going to reveal a secret. An admission. A confession of sorts. But I implore you not to jump forward to the end. The secret really won't make any sense at all without first reading all that comes before.

This is a short book with a surprise at the end. I sincerely hope you enjoy it.

Chapter Three

THE TWO WORLDS

This is a preliminary chapter that will set the scene for what's to come. It may feel like a detour, but please stick with it. There's gold in this chapter. Take this on board and it could make the difference between your success or failure with the technique itself.

In my writing and teaching, I have often used the metaphor that we seem to exist in two distinct worlds or realms. One realm is the everyday world of things and stuff, of people and jobs and responsibilities, of past and future, and of problems and solutions.

The other is the magical world of intuition, feeling, timelessness and insight.

Of course, I'm speaking completely metaphorically here. There aren't really two different worlds at all. It's the same world in both cases, just viewed differently, described differently and ultimately, experienced differently. I find this metaphor particularly helpful in explaining things, so I hope you'll be open to it.

Ironically enough, it's the magical world that is more 'real'. The everyday world of things and stuff exists only as a sort of conceptual overlay, an illusion. And if this is all starting to sound too spooky and esoteric for you, there's a really straightforward way to understand this:

The everyday relative world is made up of everything we *think* about what's here.

The magical world is what's *actually* here.

Without realising it, most of us spend almost our entire lives bewitched by an illusion. We think we are seeing what's actually here, when in fact we spend all our time thinking *about* what's here. We live in a world consisting of judgements, hopes for the future, worries about the past, and obsessing over how to make the next moment better than *this* moment. In other words, we spend almost all our lives concerned with things that *aren't even here.* And because we've been doing it for so long, we don't even notice we're doing it.

All the time we're lost in thinking about what's here, we deflect our attention away from what's *really* here. And as a result, we spend our entire lives not noticing that quieter, truer, more magical world sitting beneath all that conceptual noise and clutter. We don't see the magic right in front of us.

We only find happiness and contentment in the magical world. But because most of us don't even know it's there, we spend all our lives looking at and trying to change the wrong part. It's hard to accept that we are living in an illusion because this illusion is so convincing, so bewitching, so seemingly important. If you're particularly rational or scientifically-minded, you might even deem the magical world as a non-existent, woo-woo, fantasy world for the weak minded.

But even if we do have an inkling that there might be more to reality than meets the eye, we can't help but see the relative, illusory world of things and stuff, of hopes and dreams, of problems and solutions as being more important. At the same time, we are likely to view the spiritual realm as airy-fairy, unimportant, or maybe just as a luxury we can't afford to indulge in. After all, we must still go to work and look after our kids and pay our bills and clean our houses. We still need to deal with the trials and tribulations of ordinary life. Perhaps you'd *love* to spend more time looking at magic and spiritual growth, but you simply must sort out your material life first.

This is a mistake, but it's one we all make.

It's actually a mistake we *must* make. We must work through our seeming real world issues before we can see the truth. We have no choice. We must sort out our problems and fix our lives. This is the deal. This is the game. This is the path. And for the vast majority of people there is no shortcut. We must crawl through the mud to reach the gold.

I often explain our journey along the spiritual path as requiring us to have a 'foot in both worlds'. I teach people about magic and intuition and the truth beneath the illusion. However, at the same time, we cannot and should not ignore or deny our apparently real-world lives. In my teachings, I usually try to keep one foot in the everyday world of things and stuff, problems and solutions, and the other foot firmly planted in the magical realm.

As a result of my attempts to keep a foot in both worlds, I'll sometimes say contradictory things. You'll sometimes hear me talk in what sounds like totally rational, scientific, everyday real-world terms. And at other times, I'll fall into using the most far-out and esoteric notions. Whenever we straddle these two worlds, we come across infuriating paradoxes. Please try not to be unnerved by paradoxes, inconsistencies or contradictions in what I say. In fact, I'd urge you to be supremely unbothered by paradoxes.

Allow paradoxes to exist. Don't try to work them out. Just feel your way through them. Experience them. If you live through them, they will eventually reveal what they mean.

Paradoxes are not mistakes.

Remember, the two realms I speak of are not separate places. They are not different things. They are simply different ways of *describing* the same thing. When we are faced with a paradox, it means that we are using language to describe things that cannot easily be described with words. Paradoxes do not exist in reality, they exist only in thoughts, in words, and in language. The two irresolvable sides of a paradox don't refer to independently-existing real things. So worrying about a paradox is like worrying about the argument you had in last night's dream.

The appearance of a paradox just means that one concept is bashing up against another. Trying to resolve the situation is impossible because you're trying to reconcile two ultimately non-existent things. You're trying to find the most accurate way of placing language on top of what's truly here. But because language is completely unsuited for the job, you'll never make it fit well enough to avoid paradoxes, confusion, and misunderstanding.

Anyone who teaches from a place of real integrity ends up trying to describe the indescribable with words. Attempting to describe truth with illusion.

Placing concepts on top of something that has none. Dividing reality up into convenient parcels with words—words that *don't ultimately refer* to anything.

So there is no need to solve a paradox. In fact, you shouldn't even try...

Throughout this book, I'm going to say things that don't make rational sense. But I don't want you to see this as a problem because there is usually no need to understand what I'm saying *intellectually*. The understanding we are looking for is a subtle experience—an in-the-moment sense or feeling for what I'm talking about. An insight. An 'aha' moment. Thinking deeply and trying hard will never get you to this subtle, intuitive understanding. And I know this can be hard to accept.

It can be hard to come to terms with some of the ideas in this book. And there's a reason for that. It's hard to get your head around these ideas because you can't *think* your way to the sort of understanding we are looking for. But that doesn't stop your thinking mind having a go.

Let's take an example. What happens when you hear something like, 'the universe is one' or 'your fundamental essence is love', or 'we generate the reality we see'?

Almost certainly, you won't fully understand these statements. But your thinking mind can't help but immediately kick into gear, trying to work out what these statements mean, and passing judgement when it can't. It might say 'yes, I know that', 'I can't understand that', or 'what a load of rubbish'. But it will always say *something*. And we tend to accept what our thinking mind says as meaningful and important, without question.

In a future section, I will explain the way that we all create our own reality in every moment. As such, human beings are basically 'reality-generators'.

And I warn you now, that your thinking mind is going to be all over this statement, *you are a reality generator*. It's going to muscle its way into the middle of things, trying to work out what this could possibly mean, using all the things it thinks it already knows. And it will fail, *by necessity,* because it *doesn't* know this.

Your thinking mind *only* works with what it's seen before. It takes old, familiar thoughts and concepts and rehashes them into different combinations to create something that passes for knowledge.

So when it hears about something new and different, something it's never experienced, it essentially has nothing to work with. But that doesn't stop it. It creates *something*. And because it doesn't really know what it's doing, that particular *something* never really hits the mark. A picture, a concept appears in your head of 'reality generation' that doesn't look right, or doesn't make sense, and you feel frustrated and demand an explanation. Remember this. When you feel frustrated that you don't understand something, all it means is that your thinking mind has jumped in to interfere, but it has no business here. The thinking mind deals in certainty, reason and logic and it finds paradox intolerable. And what we are trying to describe isn't concerned with certainty, reason or logic. Those notions have no place in what we are talking about. They are completely inappropriate and unsuited for the purpose. Once you let go of logic, reason and certainty, the apparent paradoxes disappear.

It sounds intolerable to the thinking mind to let go of logic, rationality, and certainty. And if your intellect is strong, it takes a real act of courage and trust to take that step into the unknown. This is one reason why I find the notion of magic so, so powerful. You can't understand magic because *you're not supposed to*. Magic involves giving up trying to work things out. And therein lies its power. In throwing your hands into the air and saying, 'it's just *magic*' your overactive thinking mind rests, just for a moment. And when the constant conceptualising and categorising, judging and criticising *stops*, you see a chink of something else, something truer. You start to see what's actually here, not what you *think about* what is here.

When this happens, all the crazy things I say in this book will suddenly make total sense. And you'll see the truth laid bare— *You really do create your own reality.* But until then, you're unlikely to understand. You won't have any knowledge of this until you *see* it for yourself. Not until you have an in-the-moment experience of the truth of it.

Because the truth isn't found by your thinking mind. The truth is what is revealed when your mind gets out of the way.

Chapter Four

MY FAVOURITE PARADOX

In the previous chapter, I suggested that you be unbothered by paradox. And there's one paradox that comes up again and again in my work. One apparent conflict that I'm asked to explain again and again. When you accept this paradox, when you embrace it fully and live through it, it has the ability to 'superpower' your spiritual growth and your attempts to change your life. But when you fight the paradox, when you worry about it, and try to solve it, it will stop you in your tracks and scupper all your attempts to make progress.

Here is the paradox in question

- The way to make stuff happen in the everyday illusory world is to do things, work hard, master techniques and take a lot of action.

- The way to effect change in the magical true world is to do nothing to change it. It is to *let everything be okay,* just as it is.

When you can do both—taking action, doing stuff, making change, while *at the same time* letting everything be okay and being totally unattached to the results of your efforts—the results are phenomenal.

Of course, this makes no rational sense. I mean, how do we find the balance between doing things to create change, and letting everything be fine just as it is? How do we manage the paradox between trying to make something happen on the one hand, and not wanting to change a thing on the other?

The question I'm asked probably more than any other is, *how to do this?* How can you not want something you want? Why bother taking action if everything is okay just as it is?

This paradox has been in my writing since my very first books on magic. The business of *letting everything be okay* while also taking action has been there in my material life, my emotional life, *and* my spiritual life. And it's my tolerance of the paradox, my willingness to work *with* it, to experience it, and my acceptance that I *can't* explain it rationally, that has made me so successful in *all these areas of my life*.

I have, in effect, kept a foot in both worlds no matter what I'm doing. I've been walking a metaphorical tightrope, keeping the balance between magic and everyday reality. One eye on the illusion, the other eye on truth.

If you accept that this paradox—acting to change things while letting everything be okay—exists only in thought, you will find it easier to see that understanding of how to 'do' this cannot be worked out with the thinking mind.

That specific understanding can only come from experience.

It's actually very similar to learning to walk along a real-world tightrope. You can think about tightropes until the cows come home. You can ask as many questions as you like, you can read all the books about walking on tightropes, you can try to understand rationally, intellectually just *how to walk the tightrope.* However, the knowledge of exactly *how* to walk a tightrope, comes *only* through doing it. You have to get up onto the tightrope and try to walk. It is the same with this business of 'making things happen while letting everything be okay'. You only really *get* it when you *do* it. And somehow, we find we *can* do it. We *can* take action to change things while letting everything be okay, even though we don't fully understand how or why.

I made most of the big material changes to my life using magic, but before I had any real understanding of how it worked. These days, I think I have a better understanding of what's going on when I 'do magic', but it hasn't stopped the paradoxes from coming. Far from it. One of the strangest paradoxes of all is that I can now see that everything actually *is* okay, and that it always *has* been okay. I didn't need to make any of that stuff or do any of those things for it to be okay. It has been okay all along.

But I couldn't see that at first. I had to do and do and do. I had to make things happen. I needed to create stuff to teach me I didn't need it. I needed techniques that would eventually show me that techniques were never necessary. I never needed to create all that stuff in the first place, but I needed to create it in order to see that.

Paradox? Yeah, just a bit.

And *if* your journey is anything like mine, you'll need to make stuff happen too. You'll need to create stuff. You'll need to do a whole lot of creation before you can see the truth. And just perhaps, through this process of creation and discovery, you might get a wee glimpse of the true prize. This is why I offer you this, my ultimate manifestation technique. Use it, master it. Create all the stuff and get all the things.

Make your world perfect so that you can come to see the truth—that it has been perfect all along.

So let's now turn to that. Let's make this world as perfect as we can.

Chapter Five

MY (PREVIOUS) MOST POWERFUL TECHNIQUE

Until very recently, the most successful technique I knew for 'making stuff happen' was what I call 'Magic Words' or 'Telling a New Story'. It was the most successful technique I'd ever used, taught, or written about. It is the subject of my book, *Magic Words and How to Use Them*.

The Ultimate Technique presented in this current book is an extension of the original Magic Words technique. A revamp of sorts. It is like Magic Words but with more oomph.

In the pages that follow, I will refer to the Magic Words technique often, and a working knowledge of that method is most definitely going to make this book easier to follow. If you haven't already done so, you might consider reading *Magic Words and How to Use Them*, or, you could just do the free five-day video course I created to accompany that book. (Just visit www.becomingmagic.com to find out more.)

But, hey. You're here now. Reading *this* book, and to prevent you having to go and read *another* book or complete *another* course, I'm going to give a brief recap of the *Magic Words* technique now, just to lay the groundwork.

If you're already very familiar with using *Magic Words*, you could skip this chapter, but I recommend you do take the time to read it no matter how familiar you are with the *Magic Words* technique. Read it and refresh your memory. You might hear something totally new this time.

The Magic Words Technique

The Magic Words technique or 'telling a new story' starts with the premise that you are a 'reality generator'.

You create your own reality in every moment.

How many times have you heard this before in the law of attraction literature? How many times have you wished it were true but never really believed it?

I want to prove to you that *you create your own reality* isn't wishful thinking or spiritual woo. It's just the way things are. Let me help you believe it.

Okay, here goes.

As human beings, we do not see, hear or experience a true, objective, independent world. We don't even experience a *representation* of an objective, external world. What we *do* experience, most of the time, is a sort of conceptual overlay made of thought.

This is not just spooky spiritual stuff. When you look closely, you realise it can't be any other way.

Stop for a few moments and take a quick look around the area in which you're currently sitting. What do you see? Do you see furniture, rugs, tables, a television set, walls, floor? Do you see cloth, wool, wood, plastic? Do you see a mess, or do you see beauty? Do you see shapes or colours? Do you look on the view with annoyance, delight, or complete indifference?

Whatever you see, you see concepts. Even if you think you see solid objects, without your mind to separate the world into separate chunks, all you'd really see is different areas of colour, light and dark. So even the solid objects you see are concepts, beliefs, a story *about* what's here, not what's *actually* here. And that conceptual overlay is of *your own making*. You make it. You create it.

All you see is of your own creation.

What do you hear? You might not have noticed a sound at all until I asked you to consider it. But now that you have tuned in to sound, what do you hear? Do you hear a buzz of electrics, traffic noise, other people's voices? If you get really quiet, you'll notice other noises too, a hiss or hum in your ears or inside your head.

Stay like that for a bit and you might notice something odd happening.

All sounds will begin to blur into one, and there will be no sense of whether the sounds are inside or outside your head. It all just becomes one sound, everywhere.

But we almost never do this. Instead, we hear *things*, sound shapes that our mind has formed. Voices, cars, wind, the sounds of machinery, traffic, nature, and people. We hear a story *about* what's here, not what's *actually* here. We hear concepts.

All we hear is of our own creation.

If you're finding it hard to grasp this, just imagine how your dog or cat sees this same reality? What do they hear? Do they even notice the pictures on the walls or the softness of the curtains? One thing is for sure, your dog certainly *smells* the room differently to you. (It's unlikely you noticed any smell at all). Now, imagine how a fly experiences the room.

If your dog, cat, or a fly sees this room differently, smells it differently, hears it differently, who experiences the 'correct' reality? If none of them does then what *is* the correct objective reality? Do we have the correct view just because we consider ourselves the most intelligent? We certainly don't have the best sight, hearing, or sense of smell in the animal kingdom. So it's simply wrong to assume we have the most accurate experience of reality. In fact, in terms of pure sense experience, compared to a dog, ours is really rather *inaccurate*.

And that's not the only way in which our experience is less accurate than many other animals. Our clever minds, the things we believe make us *so* superior to the rest of nature, only act to distort our experience of reality.

The thoughts that run through our heads make up a set of beliefs, a sort of story. And *this story* is what we experience. We live in the story prominent in our thoughts at any given time. When that story is very fearful or negative, we suffer terribly. Some of us suffer so badly we take our own lives, over such things as broken relationships or failed businesses—things that might appear trivial to those around us. This is how horrifically inaccurate that story often is.

But what's *under* the story? What is actually 'out there' *without* these conceptual descriptions, underneath what we think *about* what's here? Have you ever stopped to wonder?

What is *actually* here?

Can we even be sure anything really exists, independent of our looking at it?

You may have heard the very famous story of the 16th century explorer, Magellan, and his first arrival on the shores of the New World. The indigenous people standing on the shore watching the arrival reportedly couldn't see Magellan's ships. They had no expectation, no belief, no way of conceptualising what was in front of their eyes. And because of this, they simply didn't see anything.

This story could be a mere myth, a legend. I did some research and couldn't find any real evidence to back it up, but there may be some truth in it. I say this because I experienced something very similar myself.

A couple of years ago, I visited my friends, Jenny and Dave, at Jenny's parents house. Jenny's parents live in a small English village and the satnav we were using didn't seem to understand the quaint and narrow country lanes around where they lived. My partner, Mike and I found it quite hard to navigate. After a lot of driving around, we finally found the road, the right house, and they were there waiting for us, and all was well.

'How was the trip,' Jenny asked. So we told them how hard it had been to find them, how the satnav didn't understand the country roads.

'Oh, it's easy,' Jenny said. 'In future, just remember to drive along the main road and turn right opposite the big church.'

'What church?' I said, 'I didn't see any church'. Jenny and Dave both laughed.

'What do you mean 'didn't see the church?' The huge one – the massive church right opposite the junction of our road.'

I hadn't seen it. As far as I was concerned it didn't exist. If I'd been required to give evidence to the police, or to a court of law, I'd have said there *was* no church. I mean, I had been looking everywhere intently, looking, looking, looking and I didn't see any bloody church.

Later that day, we took a walk down Jenny's road and out onto the main street. And there it was—the biggest flipping church I have ever seen! Almost a cathedral sitting there on its own, right opposite the turning to her road. We must have driven past it half a dozen times. It must have been in my sphere of vision, the light from it must have entered my eyes, but I just didn't 'see' it. Now that I could see it, it existed. But earlier on that day, it didn't.

I find this fascinating because it demonstrates that we don't see a true pure representation of reality, not ever. Can you appreciate that we are always seeing through the veil, the conceptual framework of objects, colours, shapes with all their uses and significance, spatial and temporal dimensions thrown in at the same time. We only ever see the bit we create ourselves, not the bit that's 'really there'. In fact, the reality we see is 100% generated by us. We truly are reality-generators.

The world is what we think it is. And what we don't see can't be said, in any worthwhile sense, to exist for us. All we can say with confidence is that there *appears* to be 'something' in front of our eyes, but we cannot *know* what that something is.

And if this sounds far-fetched then let's put all 'spirituality' aside for a moment and consider things in purely scientific terms.

According to science, what we *see* is not reality itself, but an image created in the brain after processing the light that comes *from* reality. When light from an object hits the retina, it is turned into information in the form of nerve impulses. 'Seeing' happens when that information from the retina is processed by the visual cortex and reproduced as an image. And that means *we never actually see objects*. What we 'see' is something akin to a photograph produced inside our brain, by *us*.

When we touch something, that object becomes once again turned into nerve impulses that travel up our arms, eventually being reproduced into a feeling, a texture, a physical sensation *created in us, by us*. And the same goes for all other senses. Whatever we see, touch, smell, taste and hear…is created in us and by us.

So even according to physics, we only *ever* see a *representation* of reality, and that representation is 100% constructed by us. We can't even know if what we experience is what others experience. Do I see red in the same way that you see red? Does my voice sound the same to you as it does to me? It is simply impossible for us ever to know.

Given this, we can see that the independent world is something we can only guess at, something we can only ever infer. We cannot know with our senses what is *actually* there.

But what we *can* know is that this apparently cruel and unforgiving outside world is absolutely generated by us. This is the only reality we can ever see. And even if we are sure the world exists independently of us, we can have no idea of its actual real independent nature. *If* something is 'really there' it must remain a mystery to us … for now.

Even the most rigorous scientific experiment depends upon the same perceptual apparatus of the scientists who create the experiment, do the observations, take the readings and even design the equipment used to carry it out. And this is true whether we are looking at the macro or the subatomic level. This means that none of us, not even our most advanced scientists have a clear and true understanding of an independent reality.

And if you want to get *really* sciencey about it, why not take a look at quantum physics. At the subatomic level, matter itself cannot really be said to exist at all until it is 'seen' by an observer. Until that point, it exists only as a sort of potential. A swirling mass of all possibilities. *We* turn that swirling mass of potentialities into matter. *We* make the possible actual. *We* put the objectivity into objects, the thing-ness into things. This means that, putting all the woo in the world aside for a moment, according t o *science,* the objects we see in front of our faces at this second are 100% generated by our looking at this second. We see what we generate.

So, you really are a reality-generator. Not just metaphorically, not just spiritually-speaking, but literally.

Even science says so.

Chapter Six

BELIEFS CREATE THE WORLD

So what determines *how* reality appears to us?

I've been using magic longer than I've fully understood it. These days, I feel I have a much better understanding of what underlies all I have done to change my life. As a result, my message and teachings have 'matured' over the years. But there are plenty of things about my understanding that have remained unchanged since I first started writing about magic. One of these ideas is that the experience we generate is determined by the beliefs we hold. We don't believe what we see. We see what we believe.

In other words, it's not mere *thoughts* that become things, but *beliefs*.

Beliefs dictate *how* we experience things. If I believed people were out to get me, that's largely how I'd see people. If I believed people were generally good, I'd tend to experience people that way.

What I had never realised until very recently is that beliefs don't just dictate *how* I see the outside world, *they create the world in the first place.* They don't just determine the way I see people, *they determine that there are people at all.* Beliefs create the whole lot.

Beliefs dictate *what* we see.

These are things we believe so strongly that we don't realise that they are beliefs at all. We believe our memories, and stories told by people we trust. We believe the sun is a burning ball of gas, that cushions are soft and tables are solid. These sorts of beliefs are just taken as facts, as 'what is', as 'what exists', as 'what's true'.

In the last chapter I attempted to give you a scientific explanation for the idea that *you are a reality generator.* That wasn't just a fun diversion, it was all part of the magic. Because the truth is my inclusion of this *scientific* explanation may actually make the *magic* work better.

How so?

Well, the great thing about dipping your toe into science is that it could just have the effect of helping you to believe in *The Ultimate Technique*, particularly if you consider yourself to be a very rational person. If you understand *how* the technique works, you are more likely to believe *that* it will work. And in a delightfully twisty turny circular manoeuvre, we have a situation where our belief in the effectiveness of the technique actually makes it more effective.

Put simply, if we *believe* it works, that is exactly what we will experience. And the more we believe it, the better it will work.

So beliefs *are* kind of a big deal. Because it's through the veil of beliefs that we experience the world. Or, perhaps more accurately, it's *via* the veil of beliefs that we *create* the world. Indeed, our belief that there even *is* an 'outside world' makes it appear as though there is one.

Once again, consider what you see in this very moment.

Stop and just take a quick look around the room. What do you see? A table, walls, chairs, other furniture, pictures on the wall, perhaps other people. All these perceptions depend on our belief in tables, walls, chairs and so forth. If we see a person, that person is seen through the lens of our belief that there are things called other people with lives and histories and relationships and points of view and selves of their own. But we don't actually perceive those things. We construct those notions with thought. Chairs and tables and people are *not* what's there. Chairs and tables and people are things we think *about* what's there.

So it never crosses our mind that we need a belief in people in order to see people. We just take it as read that there are people in the room.

But that's ridiculous. Of course, there are other people. The other people in the room are my husband and children. I married one of them and gave birth to the others!

Okay, now let's get very quiet and very honest here. Consider *what* you actually see in this moment. You don't see people that you gave birth to. You don't see a person you married. That information is not in this room. To come to that conclusion, you had to add in an *interpretation* of what you see. You had to refer to thoughts and beliefs about where these so-called 'other people' came from, of being a mother and a wife, of the past and to a memory of getting married and having given birth. In short, you had to refer to something that isn't actually 'in' that room.

Without those thoughts, beliefs and interpretations, all you would see, *at most,* would be a couple of skin-coloured blobs that appear to move and sometimes makes sounds. If we take away the belief we have in people, in what they are and what they do, and what they mean to us, we would be left with mere shapes and sounds. The 'person-ness', the 'my husband-ness', the 'my children-ness' of what you see in front of you is an overlay of beliefs.

The same is true of the objects like chairs and tables. *Without* belief, all you see is shapes and colours. The 'solid object-ness' is added in by you.

It's all being added in by us. All of it. All we see is conceptual overlay. All we see, hear, and touch is nothing but a veil of beliefs. Without belief, what's there is really very mysterious.

When you get *very* quiet and very still, you'll start to notice that even the different shapes, colours and sounds become indistinct and start to blur into one. Don't worry if you can't get a feel for this just yet. It's something that tends to dawn on you when you've been looking in this direction for a little while.

Chapter Seven

WHAT IS BELIEF?

So what *is* belief? What does it mean when we say we believe something?

Once upon a time, I thought 'belief' was deeply mysterious. Beliefs seemed to come from somewhere fundamental, somewhere real, going way deeper than mere thoughts. Beliefs were tied up with truth and knowledge and something inherent in my very identity. For a time, I almost felt as though I *was* my beliefs because they felt so much an essential part of me. And because they were so special, so fundamental, so determining, I imagined beliefs must be very, very hard to change.

Over the years, beliefs have become far less mysterious and spooky to me.

Beliefs are thoughts we deem to have gravity, importance, they come with relevance, with significance. In this sense, they are somewhat different to the sorts of random nonsense or fantasy thoughts that pop in and out of our heads throughout the day.

But a belief is still basically a thought. All that makes a belief 'special', all that sets it apart from any old thought, is that we think it over and over to the extent that we deem it to be true.

This means that a belief, *any* belief has no particular foundation in truth. We may think certain thoughts are true, but that doesn't mean they *are* true in any objective way. They are still *just thoughts*.

And just like any thought, a belief can change in an instant. Even fundamental beliefs held for a lifetime can come crashing down and reveal themselves to be untrue. Just ask anyone who's found out their apparently loyal and devoted spouse has been cheating on them for the past three years. Just ask anyone who's met and liked their enemy. Just ask anyone who's lost or found God.

And this immediately begs the question: if we are generating our own reality in every moment with belief, why does this reality often cause us to suffer? And if beliefs are just thoughts that can change in an instant, why don't we change them? Why do we create frightening, painful, or uncomfortable realities? Why don't we create a heaven to enjoy?

Well, here's the problem. Most of the time, we have little to no control over the beliefs we hold and thus the reality we generate.

We may have beliefs like,

I'm not good at maths, life is unfair, it's too late for me to change, I'm a weak / clever/ capable / useless / strong-minded / independent person. Some beliefs are tied up with our values and morals. I'm talking about things such as *it's important to do the right thing, women need to stand up for themselves, men need to grow up, criminals need understanding, not punishment, black lives matter.* Since such beliefs are tied up with our very identity as a good person, we might deem it wrong even to question them.

Then there are those beliefs that seem to be so fundamental they seem almost to *be* who we are. I'm talking about such beliefs as *I'm a woman, I'm a man, I'm black, I'm white, I'm gay, I'm straight. I was abandoned as a child, so I've always had a problem with trusting people. I'm a shy person so I'm better in a small group than a crowd.* These are things we would never stop to question.

Some beliefs are things that appear *so* true, that we don't even know they are beliefs. I'm talking about things like believing in a separate world, believing in time and space, believing there are solid objects, believing there are separate people. These are things we don't question. We don't consider them beliefs, but 'facts'. We consider these just things that are t rue.

And even if we *do* decide to question our most fundamental beliefs, we have no obvious way to consciously change them. I mean, have you *tried* to change your belief in time? Have you *tried* not to believe in solid objects?

But there's another difficulty in trying to change a belief. As you have certainly noticed, human beings tend to have very busy minds. We have words and pictures and complete stories running through our heads at all times. Most of these thoughts are spontaneous and pop in whether we want them to or not. Thinking happens all on its own.

But it's not all hopeless. It turns out that there are also thoughts we *do* have some control over. This can be illustrated easily if you stop reading right this second and...

... think of your absolute favourite restaurant.

What happened? I can guarantee that some images popped into your mind, and it happened spontaneously without your being able to do anything about it. But if I now ask you to describe this restaurant, or tell me about the food you enjoy there, you can do so. You can decide to think about the restaurant in a certain way. You can choose to think about your favourite meal. In doing so, you can take control of *some* of the thoughts that run through your mind. And this is where the *Magic Words* technique is so very helpful. Telling a new story with magic words rests on the assumption that by taking control of the thoughts we *can* control we can influence those we *can't*. The *Magic Words* technique or 'telling a new story' involves telling the story you would like to be true until you start to believe it. Because when you start to believe it, you will start to see it.

It probably appears that you are merely describing a life that happens in front of you. Life happens—*then* you tell a story. But if you become very quiet and honest and look very closely at your own life and the stories you tell, you might just notice something quite astonishing—life doesn't happen *to* you, and you *then* tell a story. Life is created *by* the story you tell in the moment you tell it.

So all you need do to change your life is to pick a story you would like to be true and start speaking only in terms of that story, both aloud to others and privately to yourself. Speak only as if that story were actually true. Just pick a future and talk it into existence. Command the universe with the story you tell. Literally, talk yourself into the existence you want. By doing no more than this, you can make *astonishing* things happen.

By taking deliberate charge of the thoughts you *can* control, in time, the random, uncontrollable thoughts will eventually begin to follow suit. There's no need to worry about uncontrollable spontaneous thoughts, because as long as you stick to a certain story when you can, *all* the thoughts you generate will begin to change in line with this new story.

In the free video course I created to accompany the book, *Magic Words and How to Use Them*, I advise people to pick a small niggling, everyday unwanted situation to work on. An irritating or annoying situation—an event or relationship in your life that you have trouble with, something that winds you up. Changing a personal gripe with *Magic Words* often seems to work faster than anything else, because when something has been bothering you constantly, it's very apparent when it stops. Changing a small personal niggle allows you to see the change very quickly. Consequently, this is a great way of demonstrating the power of this technique very quickly indeed.

All you need do is to start telling a completely positive story about the niggling situation while point-blank refusing to say anything bad about it. Whether you're speaking out loud or to others, you must keep to the positive story. The specific words don't matter, and they don't need to sound 100% true at this stage. But it does help if you're not telling a blatant lie. Rather, choose to say something that seems as though it *could* be true.

So if you're trying to meet the man of your dreams, don't say *I am married to a wonderful man*. No part of you is going to believe that. Instead, you might say, *there are so many wonderful men I haven't yet met. I'm so looking forward to meeting the right one for me.*

Don't say, *I am a millionaire* if you're overdrawn at the bank. Instead, you might say, *I managed to save fifty pounds this month. What a great start to my plan for financial freedom. I already feel richer.*

Don't say, *my children always tidy their room* if they haven't tidied it in months. Instead, you might say, *my children are doing their best. If I appreciate them for what they do, they'll do more of it.*

In other words, don't tell a pack of lies. Look for a little positive, true-*ish* thing to say about what is going on. This is *not* always easy at first, particularly if this is a real button-pushing situation for you. But that's kind of the point. When you can find something truly positive to say about something you really don't like, you'll be causing massive change.

So look for the gold. There will always be a little there if you look hard enough. Look for the most positive story you can tell and keep doing it. Keep steering the thoughts in the direction of a better future. Choose something that feels just true enough to help nudge your thoughts in a more positive direction.

So don't lie, *nudge*.

If we tell a story often enough and consistently enough, that story will become habitual, will become 'the norm'. And when you tell a particular story consistently and for a long time, something amazing happens. When you begin consciously, deliberately to take control of the voice in your head, to use it to tell only a positive story, *the spontaneous thoughts begin to follow suit*, and we begin to think in terms of the new story. We start to believe it's true.

And when we begin to believe the new story is true, *we will begin to see it as true in our lives*. We will begin to see the world through the conceptual overlay of the new story and the corresponding reality we see will begin to change.

This is how telling a new story with *Magic Words* works. And work, it does, often spectacularly. I've transformed my sleep, my finances, my relationships and much of my life by carefully considering the words I use. And it's the technique my readers and followers most often report as the most effective for creating change. Tens of thousands of people have changed their entire experience of life just by telling a different story.

Chapter Eight

NOT EVERYONE LOVES WORDS

Despite everything I've just described, not everyone has had success with the *Magic Words* technique. For some, it simply hasn't resonated. They haven't been able to 'grasp' quite how this works or how to use it effectively.

I suspect I know the reason why the very *language-based* technique of *Magic Words* hasn't resonated with certain people. After all, I am a writer and words are big in my world. I love language, and I write for fun. I write to help me think. I write when I'm happy and I write when I'm sad. I write when I'm feeling particularly insightful and I write when I feel thick-headed and dopy. I doubt there's been a day since about the age of ten that I haven't written *something*, if only a diary or journal entry. So I'm more just a little fond of words. And I think sometimes I have underestimated the effect this 'wordiness' has had on my view of the world and how it works. In the same way that a devout Christian can't help but see truth through the eyes of Christianity, and the way that Einstein couldn't help but see truth through the eyes of physics, I can't help but see things in terms of words.

But maybe it's not like that for you. Maybe you're more of a feeling-based person. Maybe you're visual. I've come to realise there are those of us who are less verbal, less word-based, and tend to think more in pictures or feelings. So if the whole business of *Magic Words* never particularly resonated with you, keep reading—everything might be about to get far more interesting for you.

In the previous chapter, we saw the way that beliefs create your world. Because this is something I have been aware of for a very long time, I am very familiar with examining my beliefs, changing my beliefs, and not necessarily trusting my beliefs.

I have become open to the idea that everything I believe is basically up for argument. But, perhaps like most people, I had always imagined beliefs to be purely thought-based things. And when I say thought-based, I mean I thought they lived in my head, as a sort of configuration in my brain, like some kind of data set.

But just recently I had a spectacular new insight into the nature of reality that blew everything wide open...

A belief is a thought we take to be true, yes. But they are a *little* more complex than that. I have come to realise that beliefs are not contained only within the brain. Beliefs extend out and seep into other parts of our lives. Beliefs are in our conversations, the relationships we have, the jobs we do and the whole way we conduct our lives. In fact, every conscious action and everything we choose to do is imbued with absolute and utter belief of some sort or another.

We go to work because *we believe we must earn money*

We earn money because *we believe it's necessary for a better life*

We strive for a good life because *we believe it will make us happy*

Even just walking down the road, we are the embodiment of a whole host of beliefs for example:

That we should wear clothes in public
That it's rude to stare at strangers
That we are a human individual having an individual experience within an objective world.

Our entire experience is made up of different beliefs. So beliefs are not *just* thought-based things. We could say that we see through the eyes of belief, and we hear through the ears of belief, we feel through the feelings of belief and the emotion of belief.

A belief is also in our deeds, our decisions and our actions. In fact, our *actions* may be a better indicator of our beliefs than our thoughts alone.

Beliefs are not one-dimensional. They do not reside only in the world of words or the world of thoughts.

They are in sights, sounds, feelings, emotions and action. They are, in a sense, multisensory.

And this changes everything, because if beliefs are multisensory, we don't have to limit ourselves to using words to change them.

Chapter Nine

WHERE THE ULTIMATE TECHNIQUE CAME FROM

I've been at this game for nearly twenty years. Ever since I picked up a copy of *The Power of Now*, I've been resolutely 'on the path'. The path has led me from the law of attraction, through Zen Buddhism, Neurolinguistic Programming (NLP), nonduality, and myriad different methods and techniques. I've found almost everything helpful to some degree, and I've discovered almost everything 'spiritual' has at least a grain of truth in it—as long as it's written from a place of integrity.

But there was always one technique that left me cold. One method that no matter how well-documented or highly recommended, I just couldn't master. In all my history with magic, manifesting and the law of attraction, I've always had a massive resistance to using *visualisation* as a tool for change and creation. I know loads of people get great results with it—people I trust and respect. Even sportspeople, musicians and non-spiritual types recommend visualisation as an excellent tool for personal development and change.

But not me.

You'll find very little reference to visualisation in any of my books on magic, because I only write from my own direct experience. And in *my* direct experience, I've always found visualisation boring, frustrating, and ultimately useless.

And now I know the reason for this.

I can create with words effortlessly but when it comes to my visual sense, it's a different story. When it comes to sight, I have no real creative instinct or imagination. I can barely even manage to work out what colour to paint my bathroom or what dress looks good on me. And skills that involve real visual imagination like architecture or graphic design are utterly mysterious to me. Little wonder I found visualisation such a chore.

And if this lack of visual creativity was preventing me from using visualisation techniques effectively, then might a lack of wordiness prevent others from using my magic words technique effectively?

But my lack of visual creativity is not the only reason I couldn't get visualisation to work for me. It was also that I had been doing visualisation *all wrong*.

If you've followed me for any length of time, you'll know I have often warned against treating magical techniques as if they are somehow independent of you. Techniques are not like magic wands that contain power in themselves. You cannot just pick them up and use them like waving a wand or pressing a button and watching things change. In themselves, techniques, methods, and even magic words, are completely powerless in making things happen.

Techniques only work because of their effect on yo
u. *You* are the instrument of power. *You* are the
source of the change. The magic comes only from
you.

And telling a new story is a perfect illustration of
this.

In *Magic Words and How to Use Them,* I go to some
lengths to point out the difference between telling
a new story with Magic Words and doing plain old
affirmations. To be effective, 'Magic Words' must:

1. be chosen only by you,

2. be spoken 'in that moment', and

3. tell a story you want to be true.

Magic Words are powerful *only* because they have an
effect on you, and in turn, on the reality you pro-
duce. The creation, the conceptualisation happens
instantly. So the words you use can't be predetermined ahead of time. They must be chosen according to what makes sense to you *at that moment.* And
the only one who can choose them is you. Done
'correctly', affirmations can be tremendously pow-

erful. I have had a lot of success in the past with affirmations, particularly where they concerned 'bodily' things such as pain, illness and my ability to sleep well. But I never had any luck changing the apparently outside world or other people using affirmations.

For example, I remember following Napoleon Hill's instructions in *Think and Grow Rich*. I wrote down my goal on index cards and post it notes and repeated it verbatim, for months.

And it had no effect whatsoever. Nothing.

I also repeated some of the most famously recommended affirmations about a billion times without any discernible effect. I moved from guru to guru, author to author, using different recommended - affirmations every time. Just to see which guru had the 'best' one.

Given what I now know about how *Magic Words* really work, it's little wonder that my pathetic attempts at manifestation through affirmation had no effect.

I remember continually repeating these statements that I had taken directly from others

I am succeeding in life
I know I can achieve anything I want in life
Prosperity flows to and through me
I will succeed by attracting people who can help me
I know a positive attitude can bring me abundance
I am full of vitality

But these words weren't *mine.* They were someone else's. They were pre-planned, predetermined and not chosen 'in the moment' according to the story I wanted to be true. I don't even use the words 'prosperity' or 'abundance' in my normal speech. Yet here I was, repeating them like a parrot.

No wonder nothing happened.

In *Magic Words and How to Use Them*, I explained that mindless repetition of someone else's words is likely to have little to no effect on *you* and hence little to no effect on the reality you generate. And despite everything I said in that book, it turned out this was *exactly* the mistake I had been making with visual-isation. I had been performing visualisation robotically, mindlessly, just like repeating empty affirmations. Not only that, I'd been using other people's guided suggestions, treating the technique as a chore to be got out of the way, as if the pictures in my head contained power in themselves. As if someone else's *guided* visualisation could ever work.

I was viewing visualisation like a tool in itself, something to be used, picked up and put down when finished with. As if all I needed to do was visualise a million pounds and it would appear (something I have always warned against). It became obvious. C *orrect* visualisation is as far away from my half-arsed attempt at visualisation as my *Magic Words* technique is away from dead affirmations.

Chapter Ten

CORRECT VISUALISATION

So what is the 'correct' way to do visualisation? This is where it might help if you are already proficient with using the *Magic Words* technique because it's a fairly straightforward and easy step to shift that practise to the visual sense. In other words, it's not difficult to consider what you do with *Magic Words* and apply it to visualisation too.

Telling a new story with magic words depends on your being able to 'nudge' the thoughts you *can't* control by using the thoughts you *can* control. In this way, you can influence your spontaneous thoughts, guiding them in the direction you would like them to go with the story you choose to tell.

It's very important that the words you use are chosen 'now' according to what feels more in keeping with the new story *at this moment*. They should not be decided ahead of time and formulated into a perfectly-worded statement, but should rather be flowing and natural—just like words you would normally use. *Only this time, we tell only the story we want to be true.*

When it comes to doing correct visualisation, we do exactly the same thing, only using a purely visual sense rather than words. Correct visualisation is performed by imagining, in the moment, whatever fits more in keeping with the reality we wish to *see* true. By visualising situations and images we want to occur, we can begin to affect the things we *see* in the actual world.

Once again, it is of utmost importance that this is done 'in the moment', rather than worked out ahead of time. The point of power is always *now* because all creation happens *now*. This means that using a pre-made pre-prepared visualisation script will always be less effective, and even less so if that pre-prepared visualisation script has been created by someone else.

So just like with magic words, visualised magic images should:

    1. be chosen only by you

    2. be visualised 'in that moment', and

    3. tell a story you want to be true.

And here's the exciting bit you may not have considered before. The visual sense isn't confined to imagination, 'in your mind's eye' daydreams and formal eyes-closed practices. You can also 'choose' to see certain things *with your eyes open*.

This has become the way I prefer to use the visual sense. It is incredibly powerful. For example, if you're wanting to be slimmer and healthier, look in the mirror and *choose* to see health, youth, and a slim, fit body. Look past the bits you don't like and focus only on the parts you do. A good tip for this is to see yourself as if through the eyes of someone who loves you. For example, does a doting mother look at her son or daughter and see a fat, wrinkly, tired old sack of lard? Does she see stretch marks and love handles, flab, and dry skin? No, she sees her perfect child, no matter what. Try this. Look at yourself through the eyes of love and notice the difference.

In time, you will start to see it. In time, you will see yourself as perfect.

If you choose to focus on only your partner's good points, he or she will appear beautiful to you. If you look through the eyes of someone who loves life and sees nothing but good, those things you once consciously *chose* to see start appearing spontaneously in your visual field. You will believe it. And when you believe it, you can't help but see it.

So what would you like to see happen? All you need do is visualise everything turning out in a positive way, seeing outcomes you want to happen. Not in a dead, robotic way, and not in a yearning, longing, lacking way, but in a more energetic, optimistic, commanding way, *just like we do with words*.

Visualise a new story with your eyes closed, and *see* a new story with your eyes open. In time, that story will start to come true.

But hang on a minute!

We know what incredible things can be achieved by telling a new story. We know that by taking control of the thoughts we *can* control, we can influence the ones we *can't*, so that the spontaneous thoughts, and eventually the beliefs, end up being more like the ones we want. And we also now know that the visual sense can be used to tell a new story in exactly the same way as we can do with words.

But why stop there?

Why not use the whole gamut of senses we have?

I've told you the amazing changes that take place when you tell a more positive story. You can transform every part of your life in this same way. But by focusing *only* on telling a new story with words, it's like we've only been using a fraction of the power! It's like we've been trying to run a race using only one leg.

What might be achieved if you also saw and heard a new stor, sensed a new story with your body, and felt a new story with your emotions?

After all, belief extends into the other senses too. Imagine if we used every sense the way we do words—imagining wonderful things, hearing, and seeing them in our mind's eye, and looking out for them in reality too, feeling the feelings we'd have if those wonderful things were already here *and* telling a story that they are ours for the taking?

By taking control of the sights we *can* control, we can influence the sights we can't. By taking control of the *feelings* we *can* control, we influence the *feelings* we can't. By taking control of the emotions we *can* control, we influence the emotions we can't.

We do it with words

Why wouldn't we also do it with the images and sounds in our heads?

Why wouldn't we also do it with feelings and emotions?

We could even try doing it with smell and taste.

Anyone who's read *Magic Words and How to Use Them* and put the technique into practise already knows just how effective words can be in making actual, solid, real-world change. The *Ultimate Technique* is even more powerful because this time, we aren't using just words. We are using all our senses.

In many ways, this is a more natural and obvious method for telling a new story than just using words. After all, we may be reality generators, but we don't *just think* reality into existence. We speak it into existence. We feel it into existence. We see it into existence. We emote it into existence. That's why the reality we generate is so convincing—because this whole big 3D simulation is created by *all* our senses. No wonder we believe it.

And here's another thing. You may never have stopped to consider this, but if you become quiet and try to separate each sense out from the others, it's almost impossible to do. Food looks and smells delicious. Sound is often felt as much as heard. It's not always easy to tell where sight ends and thought begins. And thought appears all tied up and intermingled with the totality of experience. Our senses blend into each other without clear cut edges or boundaries. And if you look *very* closely, it's almost as if they all become part of one whole homogenous experience.

So let's use the lot. Not just *Magic Words*. Not just visualisations. Let's talk, think, imagine, and feel the experience we want into existence.

And even that's not all we can do.

There's more. There's something we can do *so powerful* it might just be the turbo-boost that takes our dreams from wishful thinking to being right there in our experience.

Because we can also begin telling a new story with our actions.

And this might be the most powerful aspect of all. If in every moment we begin *acting* very slightly more in the direction of where we want to go, acting very slightly as if it were true, *telling a new story with the actions we take,* just *think* of the changes that would result...

Imagine acting like a confident, powerful, accomplished, and talented person. Just think how your world would change if you did *only this*.

Imagine acting like the world is a wonderful play-ground full of fun and adventure, and that each experience was a brand-new delight. Just think how your world would change if you did *only this*.

Imagine acting as though people are all basically good, kind, and loving. Imagine acting as though people can't help but like you, and that you can't help but like them in return. Just think how your world would change if you did *only this*.

It becomes as if every step we take, every movement, every breath is in keeping with the new story. We act, not as if the story is some dim and distant place we wish we could reach, but as if it's already here.

So rather than just nudging thoughts, let's nudge beliefs, let's nudge action, let's nudge the whole darned package. See success everywhere. Feel success everywhere. Act as though success is everywhere. Feel the feelings you want to feel. Visualise the things you want to see. Use every faculty to tell the new story, not just words. Use sight, sound, words, even smells, and tastes if you like. And *act as if it's true*.

This is about a sureness, a trust, a faith that allows you to command how things appear to you. This is about you moving through life with a surety of action, a conviction in the strength of your own intentions.

This is about an in-the-moment trust in the enormity of your own power.

In the beginning, it may feel as though the only part we are changing is our positive and negative judgement about things that appear in front of us, 'putting a positive spin on things' or 'looking for silver linings'. But as we become more proficient with this, we will come to realise the conceptual veil is way deeper and way more comprehensive than a positive or negative interpretation. We don't just 'add in' a veil of good or bad. It's not just the judgement of things we generate. *It's the very existence of the things themselves.* Objects, people, time and space, are all a product of belief.

And if we're generating the whole experience (which even science agrees we are), why wouldn't we do whatever we could to try make that experience a good one? Why wouldn't we attempt to alter that conceptual overlay, to alter those beliefs so that the reality we see is more like the one we want?

Chapter Eleven

THE NITTY-GRITTY – HOW TO DO THE ULTIMATE TECHNIQUE

Let's tell a new story, change our beliefs, and experience a brand-new world.

The mechanism of *The Ultimate Technique* allows us to simply tell a new story in order to change the beliefs we hold, and ultimately the reality we experience. And because we can now tell a story with all our senses, this story-telling need not be limited to words. To create a different experience, we need to influence the parts we can't control with the parts we can. And this means using our words, our imagination, our emotions, our sense of touch, and to a lesser extent, our sense of smell and taste.

So first of all, just ask yourself, what do you want to *see*? Out of all the million billion things they could see, what do you want your eyes to show you? How do you want your conceptual overlay to appear? What visual reality do you want to generate? Riches, your children being happy and successful, better living conditions, more confidence, looking younger, being slim and healthy, maybe even being more attractive to other people?

Or maybe you just want to see yourself as happy.

So what's next? How do we tell a story with sight? Obviously, we can sit down and visualise things a structured way. In our mind's eye, we can see the future we would like to be true.

I don't recommend using a pre-recorded script or guided meditation for this process, even if you have created it yourself. Instead, I suggest you try sitting down in a quiet place with no preconceptions, no prearranged ideas about what to think, and with only a rough basic intention of what you want to create.

Then visualise *in the moment,* how you want things to go. If you want money, close your eyes, and visualise money flowing to you, not silly banknotes fluttering their way to you—that's just pure fantasy and you'll never influence belief that way.

Instead, imagine properly receiving money for services rendered in a believable way. Imagine what people will say to you. Imagine the steps you'll take or the things you'll do to make people want to give you money. Treat it as though you're planning the way the money will come to you in a fair, *believable* exchange. Remember, belief is truly powerful, and if your story is already believable—rather than pure fantasy—you'll get better results.

Personally, I prefer to visualise a general sense of 'everything being brilliant', rather than anything too specific. I've always found it more difficult to create a *particular* belief or a *particular* outcome than to create a belief that things are just going to be generally amazing. So I don't tend to focus on the specific thing I want to happen. I find that tends to act as a sort of restriction on what's possible, cutting off my access to even better or alternative outcomes.

So, instead of visualising one specific outcome, I imagine life being perfect. And because I don't tend to separate the visual sense from the auditory sense, I bring in sounds at this point too. For example, I begin imagining the sounds of joy in my family's reaction to receiving good news or birthday presents, or the sound of someone telling me I've done well. I imagine jumping for joy, elation, relief, and everyone around me smiling, congratulating me, thanking me, and being as joyful and thrilled as I am. I might also imagine myself taking steps towards what I want, but in a general way, feeling how good it would be to be going about my day with everything slotting into place.

That's how it works for me. Your mileage may vary. So if you want to experiment with visualising very specific outcomes, please do try that.

Formal eyes-closed visualisation isn't the only way we can use sight and sound. When images and sounds pop into your head, you can attempt to steer them in a direction you'd like them to go. When you think of your children, always imagine that they are happy. When a worry arises, tell a more positive story, *see* and *hear* a different future.

We can also, to some extent, take control of what we see with our eyes open and what we hear in the surrounding environment. To get a sense of this, just look around the room or the area in which you are currently sitting.

Can you see:

Shapes, colours, blobs of light and dark

Wood, metal, wool, plastic

Chairs, tables, carpets, sofas

Work, café, train, bedroom

Dump, haven, 'my special place'

My crappy life, my incredible life, my pure existence.

In any given moment, there aren't only a million billion different sights to see, there are also a million billion different *sounds* to hear—words spoken by others, buzzes, hums, rumbles, clicks, crashes, beeps and shushes. But *we* are the ones who turn this random sea of noise into cars, television sets, radios, people, microwave ovens, clocks.

It can be really effective to use our senses to *look for* things we want to see, *listen* for things we want to hear. To do this, look around in the space where you are and see what you like *best* about this room. If it's the rug on the floor, next look and see what you like *best* about the rug. When you look in the mirror, decide to see *only* your good points.

You can also choose to interpret the noises you hear in a positive way. If there's music playing, don't judge it as 'modern tuneless racket', 'irritating jazz' or 'boring classical'. Instead, we can think about what we like best about it. Find something good to say or think, listen to the sounds with as little negative judgement as possible. Let it be okay.

Do the same with voices. If someone says, 'I feel very disappointed by the way you acted', you can choose to hear that in all sorts of different ways. You could choose to hear it very negatively. Or you can choose to see it as honesty, bravery and as a desire to improve a relationship. See it as a sign of a true friendship.

Of course, for those of you who have a particularly strong sense of smell or taste, you could also do the same with those senses. Pick up your asparagus, okra, or shellfish (three things I happen to detest!), and try to smell and taste something delicious when you smell and taste them. This might be helpful if you are trying to develop a taste for a particular healthy food. Just ask yourself, *what do I like best about what I'm experiencing?* What's good here?

If you're trying to lose a taste for chocolate, put it in your mouth and consider the clawing, sticky over-sweetness. Really try and dislike what you taste.

You really can tell a new story with all your senses. You can:

- use the thoughts you *can* control to influence the ones you *can't*

- influence the images you *can't* control by using the images you *can*

- influence the sounds you *can't* control using the sounds you *can, and*

- influence the tastes and smells too.

But there's one sense we haven't mentioned yet. And that's the sense of touch and feeling. I'm going to include *emotional* feeling here, because it can be very difficult to separate emotion from physical bodily sensation.

The sense of feeling is possibly the most fun, most effective and most powerful sense in your arsenal. Just like with all the other senses, you can influence the *feelings* you can't control by manipulating the feelings you can. But feeling is far easier to control than sight or sound. Not only that, feeling is the sense with the power to dictate the course of all the other senses. We could say that feeling is primary or fundamental. Take control of the feelings alone, and everything else may fall into place.

So let's try this.

Right in this moment, what do you want to feel? If you're not sure, just ask yourself:

What do I want to experience? How would that feel?

Feel that.

Feel how it would feel to be rich. Feel how it would be to be slim. Imagine yourself happy and really feel that in the moment. Imagine how you would feel if all your dreams came true, and feel that. Get an in-the-body-right-now sensation of how it *might* feel to have everything you ever wanted. What do you want most in the world? Think of something real-world, as in, something form-based.

I want a big house with my family living nearby.

How would that feel?

I don't know.

Just try. You can't get it wrong. Let the smile spread across your face knowing it's yours. In this moment, feel it. Blankly ignore the voice in your head telling you that you can't have it. That negative voice has nothing useful to add here. Sink into the place where the feeling resides. Drop into the space that always feels good.

No matter where we are and what is going on for us right now, we *can* always choose to feel a little different. Even in the worst possible scenarios and during the most upsetting events, we can choose to feel a little different. We all can. We know how to do this. We know where the better feels are.

Go there now. Don't think about it. Don't try and work it out. Trying will get in the way. This is utterly instinctive and non-intellectual. Ignore whatever thoughts are popping in and just go to the place inside that's always at rest. Go to the place inside where everything is okay. Go to the place inside you that's content and at rest in this moment. Don't think. Just go there. Go to that place. You won't get it wrong.

Feel the Magic.

Chapter Twelve

NO NEED TO SEPARATE THE SENSES

It can get a bit confusing when we suddenly have five senses to deal with. In light of this, I encourage you not to get too contrived or specific about working on each of the individual senses. Don't stop to work out *what* to hear or *what* precisely to feel or *what* precisely to see. Don't worry about whether you should be using sight rather than sound or that you've left one sense out. Certainly, don't imagine you should be working on sight, then working on sound, or that you should be ignoring or pushing away one sense when working on another.

It's actually somewhat artificial to separate these senses into sound, sight, feeling and thought in the first place. The more attention you pay to what you see, hear, and feel in the moment, the more you'll realise that these senses don't come in discrete packets. Thoughts come with feeling, words come with pictures, and sights almost always come with sounds.

But never fear because I'm going to make the whole thing far easier for you. There's a *much* easier way of mastering *The Ultimate Technique*. A method that eradicates the confusion of working out *what* to think, say, see or feel.

We access the right feelings, sights and sounds by means of *questions*. By asking questions of ourselves, we can let our senses do the work. Ask the right questions and our thoughts, feelings, ears, and eyes will fill in the blanks for us.

The Questions

Here are some brilliant questions to ask yourself when using the *Ultimate Technique*.

What if you *knew* everything was really, *really* okay right now? How would that look? How would that sound? How would that feel? *Feel that.*

What if you were blissfully happy right now? How would that feel? *Feel that.*

If you feel a sense of lack and longing when you think of what you want, just ask yourself:

How would it feel if that feeling of lack was gone. How would it feel if that longing wasn't there? *Feel that.*

What if everything was shockingly more simple than you ever realised? How would that look, sound, feel?

What if everything you're already doing is *exactly* what you need to do to get your perfect house or partner or situation or job? How would that look, sound, feel?

What if you knew *exactly* what to do from this point on? How would that look, sound, feel.

And here's a big one:

What if you knew every action you took from now on was 100% correct? How would that look, sound, feel?

And allow your actions to follow suit. If you don't like what's going on, do something, take action, take steps to move you in the direction of your new story. Walk the way you think a rich person would walk, move your body like a slim person, hold yourself the way a happy and confident person would.

Act differently, do things in accordance with your new story. Take steps as if the story were true or coming true.

Visualise it, feel it, hear it, do it, see it, *have* it.

If you don't like what you feel, feel something different

If you don't like what you see, see something different

If you don't like what you hear, hear it differently

Whatever it is you want to experience, consider how that would feel, how that would look, how that would sound.

Imagine it... and you'll come to see it.

Speak that way... and you'll come to believe it.

Feel that way.... and you'll come to experience it.

Act that way... and you'll eventually have it.

Can you grasp this concept?

It's like a *command* to the universe to slot into place according to your will. It's a decision:

This is just how things are now.

Chapter Thirteen

IT WON'T BE INSTANT

Now, just like with words, the first few times you try and see or feel a different reality, it's all going to feel like one big lie. You're going to look at your bank balance and it's going to look just as crappy as it ever did. You're going to get on the scales and not see the weight you want to be. You're going to look at your poky little home and not see the big house. So don't start with trying to change bank balances by looking at them, or weighing 120 pounds or by picking lottery numbers correctly.

Start with, for example, seeing yourself as a little thinner, seeing yourself as a little younger, start feeling a little richer. Start with feeling yourself as happy and confident. See and feel yourself as getting this right, as being powerful and competent with magic.

Speak, imagine, and feel according to the story you would like to be true, *and do it in the moment.* Do it *according to what feels, looks, or sounds nicer in that moment.*

And I cannot emphasise this enough:

Start seeing the good aspects of your current situation.

Complain about your current situation and you'll create more to complain about. See the good in your current situation and you'll see more good stuff. It's by feeling, acting, and thinking as if what you want is already here that you will create the fastest results. And that means being 100% okay with what you already have.

Don't expect instant results, and don't let a setback stop you. Keep going. And remember, we are doing *magic* here. Magic makes life effortless, easy, light, and free. But it takes bloody hard work to master. It takes effort to reach that place of effortlessness.

This will be much easier if you bear the following in mind:

It's when you're challenged that you have the greatest opportunity for magic. It's when things are apparently going wrong that you have the greatest opportunity to put them right. It's when things apparently need changing that you can best take action to change them.

After all, any fool can tell a positive story when things are going well. Anyone can give a favourable interpretation when everything is favourable. Anyone can take action when action is obvious and easy. But when things are challenging... that's when the invitation presents itself—to do something *different*, something magical. This is when the men and women step away from the boys and girls. This is when the magically powerful come into their own. This is when you have a choice to buck the trend, go against the grain, and do something *so* different to the norm that reality can't *help* but move with you.

Still look fat? Then keep seeing yourself as thinner. Overdrawn at the bank? Then keep feeling yourself as richer. Had an argument with your partner? Then keep seeing their good points. Explain everything that happens in terms of the new story. And *act accordingly*.

Sooner or later, there will be a halt in the old way. A staging post. A pause in the fabric of space and time. A tipping point. And from there, you'll start down the road to a new future. The new story just starts looking truer. Things start to change. Everything gets easier. It starts to snowball. The momentum kicks in.

And a new reality comes into being.

Chapter Fourteen

THE REVAMPED EVIDENCE JOURNAL

Here's just one last little thing you may want to add to your reality-creation endeavours.

Consider keeping an evidence journal. In the past for me, this has proved to be an amazingly powerful technique for creating specific results. It consists of keeping a written record of all the evidence I see that proves my intended results are happening.

The evidence journal technique is based on the assumption that if you look around for evidence that something is true you will see it. The more you see evidence, the more you will believe it. And when you believe something, it will become true in your experience.

This is how I have successfully used an evidence journal:

I use a small notebook for this, around the size of a mobile phone. Each day, I simply decide on the state of affairs I wish to happen, and write that at the top of a new page. I then look around for evidence that this state of affairs is true. And in my evidence journal, I record that evidence to support the new belief in the thing I wish to see happen. I write at least three pieces of evidence per day. I find that if I really hunt around or think hard, I can *always* find evidence. And that evidence doesn't need to sound convincing or solid to anyone but me. Sometimes the evidence can be very flimsy, contrived even. For example:

My shampoo was way cheaper than usual. That's definitely a sign that I'm on my way to becoming a millionaire.

I completed all my emails in record time. This is turning out to be a very powerful day.

I have a small feeling of optimism today. I'm definitely beating this depression.

I've had a really good idea for some new marketing, a sure sign that my business is on the up.

I felt a real sense of determination to travel today. I am definitely overcoming this fear of flying.

An evidence journal is a great way to formalise what we are doing in telling a new story. The practice of writing things down like this really keeps that story at the forefront of our mind and helps us to remember to keep on telling it, feeling it, seeing it. And if you hate writing, you could always speak your evidence into a note-taking device or app.

This evidence journal need not be limited to a formal technique completed three times a day. You can get into the habit of doing this all the time, looking for evidence all the time, noting the evidence, speaking it out loud, feeling it in your body, feeling the sense of delight and satisfaction when a new bit of evidence is found.

If you think about it, looking for evidence is just another form of telling a story.

Now think how powerful this would be if you also wrote down feelings, if you wrote down things you'd seen and heard.

And think how much faster things would change if you did it in every moment of the day—mentally noting evidence *all the time*.

Just think how different your life would be if you did all we've talked about.

How fast would your belief change if you visualised what you want to see, if you felt what you want to feel, if you saw evidence all the time, all over the place that it's already here? How different a reality would you create?

The reality generator is faithful, and it is reliable. It will do as you command. It does not make mistakes. It will create exactly whatever you believe, just as it is doing so right in this very second. Whatever you see, hear, and feel in this moment... you are creating it. Grasp that. Get quiet until you reach the acute intimacy of this point. Come to now.

Realise that in *this now*, you are seeing exactly... w
hat... you... believe.

Chapter Fifteen

LET'S GO DEEP

The Ultimate Technique is not about imagining stuff you want in a separate, external world, and then expecting those thoughts to attract that stuff to you. This is about changing *you* and your beliefs so that the world you create with those beliefs is more like the one you want. This is about upgrading your reality generator using all your faculties rather than just words in order to powerfully affect the reality you generate.

We've already heard of the importance of telling your new story, 'In the moment'. That means *now*. This now. Simply put, if it's not there *now* in our experience, it's because we haven't generated it. The world does not move independently of us.

This is a point that is easily misunderstood. I have noticed that when a person can't get manifestation techniques to work for them, it's very often because of this misunderstanding. The misunderstanding may arise just because we've never slowed down enough to notice 'the now'—that silent still place at the heart of every moment.

So let's do that, *now*.

Let's just slow down for a moment or two, and notice what's actually here. It's a quiet place, and it can even feel a little dull at first. Neutral. Like a nothingness. But that silent still place is one of bursting, infinite potential.

This silence at the heart of every moment is akin to the nucleus of an atom ready to be split. Like the moment before the big bang. It is literally the moment before an entire universe comes into being. The infinite nature of this space means that the fate of the next second is entirely open, free. From here, from now, literally *anything* could appear, anything could come next. The possibilities for what the next second will be are literally infinite.

And the coolest thing of all? *You* are the one who collapses those infinite possibilities into *one* actuality. *You* turn possible to actual. Again, and again and again, the universe is created from nothing. *By you.* Without you, there is no universe. You create the entire universe in every moment, from nothing.

Not woo. Science.

Ever wondered why:

things keep turning out the same way?

your train always turns up three minutes late?

it's always the same barista serving you coffee in the café you always visit before going into the job you've hated for the past eight years?

It's because you keep creating the universe in exactly the same way. It's because the beliefs you see through and the story you tell dictate how your next second will be. And you keep telling the same story. Same story, same world. Different story, different world.

Now, what makes this difficult is that much of this story is unconsciously told. The story is in the expectations we have, the beliefs we hold and the concepts we see through.

You go out in the morning with a fully worked out idea of that job, that train, that journey to work, the barista who serves your coffee. You expect to see the same thing every day to such an extent that you don't even know that concepts and belief are involved.

Some of these beliefs (such as the belief in space, time, solid objects, and other people) are so convincing it seems impossible that they could ever not be true. As far as you are concerned, you aren't seeing beliefs and concepts, you are seeing reality, people, real objects moving in real time.

Beliefs and concepts are the reason you see solid objects instead of colours and shapes, or even just energy. Beliefs and concepts are the reason you see a train rather than metal and glass. Beliefs and concepts are the reason you hear traffic rather than a random rushing sound. They are the reason you see and hear anything at all. What is *actually* there is deeply mysterious. We may never know what is there prior to our conceptualising it. But one thing is certain, *we* are the ones who add the 'thingness' to things, the 'train-ness' to trains, the 'objectivity' to objects.

So what do you do? You are in *this* moment. Perhaps feeling stuck, feeling lost, feeling trapped in a life you want desperately to change, with each moment feeling just like the one before.

Well, we know these objects, these sights and sounds, this reality will never substantially change, unless *we* change. We know there is infinite potentiality in this moment. We know the future, the next moment, is essentially up for grabs.

And the question you probably most want the answer to is,

How can I make the next moment turn out the way I want? How can I change the future?

Now, let's slow things down even more. Let's look exquisitely closely at this 'now' thing.

If you get quiet enough, you'll notice something odd. The past is nowhere, and the future never comes. There *is* only now. One now. It is always now. It starts to feel as though life is not actually a series of moments in time, but just one single moment. And if this is true, there is no point in trying to change the future. None. Because that future never comes.

'Now' is timeless and it's always here. It's always 'now'.

So in answer to the previous question, the way to change the future is this:

Act, speak, think, and feel as if what we want to experience is already here.

Not in the future. Not somewhere else. But already here. *Now!*

Because, in a very literal way, it *is* already here. Every possibility is already here. It's your job to turn it from potentiality to actuality. It's your job to collapse the waveform of energy into matter and you do so *now*. The only point of power is always now. This now. Right now.

So this, guys, is the *real* law of attraction. This is how we *really* manifest things. Forget all that nonsense involving thinking about things you haven't got in the hope that you will somehow 'attract' them to you in the future. By thinking about something you want, all you're doing is creating a situation where you're thinking about something you want (and, by definition, not *having* it).

What I'm talking about is far more 'immediate' than that. This is about your power of conceptualisation in the moment. In every moment, you have the power to create a whole universe out of nothing. And you're doing exactly that, *now* and *now* and *now*.

You are *that* powerful.

Chapter Sixteen

COMPLAINING AS CREATION

The fact is, we're creating reality *whether we like it or not*. Constantly. We are creating the whole bloody lot of it. All the time.

When we fully appreciate this fact, it tends to have a profound effect on the way we conduct our lives. Let's see one example of that now.

If you've read any of my books, you'll know the big deal I make about the business of not complaining. The simple act of refusing to complain makes life easier, happier, more successful, and more fun. Many of us have an experience of the way that life seems to pick up and become more enjoyable when we take steps to stop complaining. And when this is done consistently and with commitment, not complaining gives you a life where there is simply nothing to complain *about.*

Refusing to complain can sound like a way of sugar-coating the world, turning a blind eye to the genuinely bad things that occur. It seems like a wilful refusal to face reality. From what we've learned so far, we can now see this as nonsensical. We don't refuse to complain because we can't face the horrible reality of a situation. We don't complain because by doing so we *create* that horrible reality in the first place.

This can get rather provoking because it can seem to imply that we are blaming the unfortunate for their misfortune. That we are blaming the victims for their victimhood.

The implication is that the reason you see a life of misery, difficulty, hardship, and disappointment is because you have made it that way. Conversely, the reason you see a life of love, riches, happiness and fun *is because you made it that way.* And it may sound disrespectful, insulting, or uncaring to suggest this.

Here's the thing. *If* you fully accept that you are creating your own life, it means the only one with the power to change it is you.

This means it can be changed!

It also means you don't have to *wait* for your life to pick up. You don't have to *wait* for someone else to fix it. You can start taking steps to improve your life, right now.

How exciting is that?

A keystone of my work since the very beginning has been the idea of taking responsibility for your entire life. Indeed, the belief that I am *entirely responsible for my life and always have been* is possibly the first great insight I ever had. This insight helped me begin the long slow journey out of the blackness of poverty and despair into magic.

When I believed my life *wasn't* my responsibility, I suffered terribly. This is because I believed it was for someone else to fix things, change things and make everything better. I believed there were myriad negative causes of my misfortune. *Things over which I had no control.* When I believed this, I was a victim. Once I saw that I could take responsibility for *all* of it, all victimhood evaporated, and I became empowered.

But I digress.

I've actually brought up this business of taking responsibility for another reason. There is something very interesting to be learned here. If you view the suggestion that *we create our own reality in every second* as disrespectful, hurtful, or plain false, that's how it will sound to you. That's how the situation will appear to you. *And that's the reality you will create.* 'Genevieve is disrespectful, insulting and hurtful' will be true for you.

Someone else, reading these same words may judge them as empowering, uplifting, motivating, truthful. This is how the situation will appear to them. This is the reality *they* will create. 'Genevieve is inspiring, she speaks the truth' will be true for them.

Insulting, false and hurtful, or empowering, uplifting, and true? Which is correct? Can you see there is no objective truth to the matter? Can you see there is no objective *truth* to the matter?

'You have created your own experience of life.'

How you hear this statement is determined *only* by your own beliefs. So the question of which view is more correct doesn't really make sense. This is not a question of who's right or wrong, because there is no external yardstick to measure against. No independent judge is possible. No objective authority exists. There is only the way it appears to you.

This is only ever a question of *what works best, what gives you a nicer experience of life?*

Perhaps you feel the nicer experience of life comes from believing I'm a disrespectful idiot. If so, that's absolutely fine. But it would probably be best to put this book down and read another. On the other hand, if you find what I've said motivating and uplifting, let's continue, because there's something very significant to be noticed here.

Any act of complaining, even the complaint, *Genevieve is a disrespectful idiot*, is a judgement. It's a form of conceptualisation. It's an act of creation itself. It's the collapsing of potential and possibility into actuality—a contraction of fluid, pure reality into a *thing*. In this case, a complaint-worthy *thing*. Something bad, something wrong, something hateful.

Hating something is really no different to calling something a table or a chair. When you call something a chair, you collapse pure potential into a neutral object of utility. But when you call something hateful, you collapse pure potential into something hateful. When you complain, you collapse reality into parts. And that to which you apply your complaint collapses into something you can't help but see as bad, as a problem, as negative.

So the truth is this. Every judgement, positive or negative, is nothing more than a new creation. When you complain, you create something to complain about. When you hate, you create something hateful.

And the almost bewilderingly significant upshot is this:

If you don't conceptualise things as problems, you will have no problems. If you don't complain, you will have nothing to complain about.

And if you let everything be okay, then it *will* all be okay.

Boom!

Chapter Seventeen

TAKING IT ONE STEP FURTHER

Why don't you have all you want? Why are you always searching? There is actually only one reason. The only reason you don't have everything you want right in this second is because you have placed a condition on having it.

You believe you will be happy *when* you buy your own house, *when* you have children, *when* you cure your depression, *when* you find a girlfriend, *when* you get over your problems, *when* you become spiritually enlightened, *when* you pay off your debts.

And while you believe *any* version of 'I'll be happy when...' *you will remain unhappy*. Why?

While you believe, 'I'll be happy when...' you keep searching for that happiness. And while you keep searching, you keep looking right past everything that's right in front of you. The truth is, everything you've ever wanted is here now, this now. And the *only* reason you don't see it is because you don't believe it's here. You don't believe it's here, so you simply don't see it.

Those conditions you think must be fulfilled before you can be happy *are actually standing in the way* of happiness. I'm not referring to the content of the conditions but the fact there are conditions at all. If you don't think in terms of conditions that must be fulfilled before you can achieve everything you've ever wanted, there will be nothing in the way of your having everything you've ever wanted. It's believing in these conditions that stops everything you want being available to you *in this moment*.

I don't have any of those sorts of conditions. But the life I want is still not here.

And there it is: the judgement, *the life I want is not here.*

That specific judgement is making this tricky for you. You have judged happiness as 'not here', therefore you don't experience it as being here. That judgement creates the condition of happiness 'not being here'.

You're judging this moment as 'not okay' and so 'not okay' is how you're experiencing it. Do you see? Your conceptualisation *in this moment* actually collapses the potential into actual. You're creating the whole thing in every second. So when you assume 'what I want is not here', you place an artificial boundary around reality, and you create a situation where what you want isn't here yet.

Drop the judgement, *I'll be happy when...*

Drop the judgement, *the life I want is still not here.*

Drop the judgement, *this isn't it.*

And what happens? Something amazing.

Literally anything and everything is suddenly up for grabs. Everything is open to you. Every possibility. Ultimate infinite potential. Good, bad, wanted, unwanted, the lot. They are all here now. And to experience something you *want* all you need do is conceptualise what is here into something wanted.

So every time you tell a story *that* you don't have what you want, *how* you're going to get what you want, and *why* you don't have it yet, you make a judgement—'it's not here yet', 'this is not okay', 'I still haven't found what I'm looking for'. And in doing this, you effectively keep what you're looking for from you. When you stop telling that story, you'll be astonished at what you find.

Everything you want is *automatically here.*

Let everything here be okay, *and it all will be okay.*

Stop searching, and *you'll find everything you're looking for.*

Pure Magic.

Chapter Eighteen

IT'S TIME TO TELL THE TRUTH

This is the sixth book I've written on the subject of creating a better experience of life using magic, and it may well be the last. I'll almost certainly write more books that result in generating nicer experiences of life, more joy and less suffering. This won't be the last book I write about magic, but I doubt I'll write another that deals with how to use magic to make *specific* things happen. This book may well be my 'last hurrah' in terms of manifestation.

And here, at the end of the book, I have an admission. A secret to tell. This secret might not be easy to stomach, understand or accept. But for the sake of my own integrity and peace of mind, and for the sake of anyone who might already be 'seeing through' what I have written so far, I offer this.

The contents of this book reflect the pinnacle of my *current* understanding. I say *current* because understanding is not a fixed or static thing. In the past, I always thought I had a pretty good grasp of what was going on. But even so, I've often found myself looking back to a past time and finding I've written things that *just don't look so true anymore*.

And the chances are, it's going to happen again. What I think and say and write today in this book will all be replaced in a few years, by a newer, more 'mature' view of what I think is *really* going on. In fact, it's already happening.

I'm in a strange and unique position at the moment of almost being able to watch as one view of the world is gradually being replaced by something new—something very different. And almost everything I've said in this book has already been superseded by a newer understanding.

That's not to say you won't find the concepts in this book immensely helpful and effective, it's just not an accurate representation of how things actually work. On the one hand, *The Ultimate Technique* I describe here 'works'. But on the other, it's not 'correct' or 'true'. It's a good and effective way of doing things, but it's perhaps not the best way of doing things.

So why on earth don't I give you that *best* way of doing things?

It's because the *absolute best* way of doing things isn't easy, doesn't make a lot of sense and probably doesn't sound very attractive to many people.

Here's the thing about this business of making stuff happen, fixing the world, changing things, and generating a better reality. We make stuff happen in order to fix problems, get the outcomes we want, change the world for the better so that we can be happy, content, fulfilled, peaceful. But no matter how much we change the external circumstances of our life, no matter how perfect we get our finances, our relationships, our living conditions and even our mental health, it will never be enough.

Despite having created all your wildest dreams, you could still have many, many moments of bleak misery. You could marry the perfect person, have the perfect children, all the money in the world and there would still be that nagging sense that something was missing.

And this is true, *without exception.*

We constantly continue trying to get things *right* so that we can feel good, but we never *quite* succeed. As soon as we get one thing we want, that wanting engine just fires up once more and we're off again, *fixing the world.* But it takes a long, long time to realise and fully accept this. And until we see the truth, we will continue to work on fixing the wrong bit. Most of us spend our entire lives in a state of wanting, looking to a future moment, when the world is fixed, when our problems are solved, our kids are happy, our bank accounts are full, and our relationships are harmonious—an elusive time *when everything will be okay.*

And so, we never get to rest, to finish, to reach that elusive end point. Instead, as Thoreau famously put it, we spend almost all our time on this planet *living lives of quiet desperation.*

One day, we think, will we rest. *One day,* we will stop. *One day,* our work to fix the world will be done. And finally, *then* we will be happy. But that time never comes. It can't. Because that's just not where happiness comes from.

Happiness isn't in the external world. Happiness doesn't come from fixing or changing the external world. Happiness isn't even affected by the external world.

Happiness is what we feel *automatically* when we stop trying to fix the external world.

Happiness does not come from getting what we want.

Happiness comes from the stopping of *wanting.*

And the only reason we feel happy when we get something we want is that this almost continual, exhausting discomfort of *wanting* suddenly, briefly, stops.

At some point, this becomes blindingly obvious. But we can't see it until we see it. And until we see it, it will look absolutely and obviously true that the world needs to be changed, that things need to improve and that we can and should take steps to make our lives better. We will continue to try to create a better life, we will continue striving for more, for different. And, if we're fans of self-help, we'll look for techniques to help us make that world *just right*. What I've offered in this book is, in my experience, the very best of those techniques.

And in doing so, I'm really straddling that paradoxical tightrope now. I really do have a foot in both worlds. Because on the one hand, I'm showing you how to get what you want, and on the other, I know that's not going to fix things.

Getting what you want is, at best, a sticking plaster, a temporary 'high'. At worst, it's a dangerous trap.

You see, in our attempts to 'fix' the apparently external world in order to feel better, perhaps by using the technique in this book, we stay pointed in completely the wrong direction—towards the world. And these 'real-world activities' take us deeper and deeper into the story-based thought world. So, while we *think* we're making our lives better, all we're really doing is effectively playing around in an illusion. We're using thought to fix thought with thought.

And I'll stop there...

This is a rabbit hole that goes on for miles. And the purpose of this book won't be served by travelling much further down it. For now, I'll just offer this:

There is an alternative. There is an alternative to manifesting things and getting our lives just so, and making stuff happen and changing the world. There is a truth to replace the lie I have described in this book.

There is another, very different way to create a life of real happiness, lasting joy, peace and ease in a way that doesn't feed into the illusion. There is a way that points you slightly more in the direction of genuine, lasting happiness.

This is the 'better' way I didn't feel able to tell you about earlier in the book. And even now, at the end of the book, you still might not like the sound of it much. Because what I'm talking about does not involve *making things better.* The truth is that attempting to create certain specific things or particular outcomes is not the best way to go about getting a better life.

In all my books and all my courses and pretty much whenever I speak, you'll hear me make a big deal of what I call 'letting everything be okay'. The way to get a better life is to allow everything to be 100% okay, to allow things to turn out however they will. And here's the amazing, magical thing—the more you can do this, the better your reality will be.

So maybe it's just time to accept the world itself and all its things and events. Maybe the way to change the world for the better is to *stop trying to change it!* To see it's already perfect. To let it all be okay, just as it is. Maybe the secret to getting everything you want is to be *okay with everything you have.*

And the answer to the question, *how do we change the world we create for the better* has to be, *we stop trying to change the world.* We don't push any of it away. We live every second, fully. We see what's here, without any attempt to change it. We let it all be, just as it is.

Now, the ultimate version of this has to be letting everything be *totally* okay, like *totally* okay, just as it is. Right now. Because the more you can accept this moment as perfect, the more perfect the next one will be.

So stop. Get quiet.

In this moment, all possibilities exist.

The only way to ensure the *next* moment is perfect is to recognise that *this* moment is already perfect.

And this has to be true because this moment and the next moment are really one. There *is* only this moment. It's all one moment. Stop trying to change it. Let the innate perfection of reality show itself. Notice that things are perfectly capable of turning out perfectly well without our trying to make them turn out our way.

How can this be? It's because if left to its own devices, everything always *does* turn out well. If not judged negatively, everything fundamentally *is* okay.

It is okay by default. The fundamental nature of reality is utter perfection. Only our judgement makes it appear otherwise.

Everything we want—all the good feelings and all the good stuff—is here waiting for us in this very minute. It's already here. We just have to let it in. We let it in by:

Stopping the search

Stopping wanting

Surrendering

Letting everything be okay

Leaving everything be, just as it is

And then, the whole thing will reveal itself to us.

This is how manifestation works. It's not about thinking of the stuff you want, or getting an energetic match with money or any such thing. It's about 'aligning' yourself with the present moment—the moment where anything can and does happen, where everything you want is already here waiting for you.

This is why we get what we want *or better,* when we let everything be okay. We tend to experience 'good stuff' when we let everything be okay, but *not* always specifically what we asked for. This also explains why other parts of our lives pick up, while the one thing we are working on may remain elusive.

So methods and techniques like the one I've described in this book can and do work, but they really work because they make this moment feel better. They only work because they help to get you closer to that magical potential-state, that perfect 'now' where everything you're looking for truly lives.

Telling a new story must be told in the moment because *it only works in the moment.* When the moment feels okay, we release our desperate attempts to control and change it. Let it all be okay, and it all *is* okay. It's more than okay. It's perfect.

The whole shebang, the whole spiritual journey has always only been about one thing. Something so fundamental, it eventually eclipses, replaces, and takes over everything else we try to do along the way. And the truth is, I've written an entire book telling you how to carry out a particular technique, how to manipulate your world to make it more like the one you want, but you could get just as good or better results by doing none of this at all. You could do one simple thing instead.

Let everything be okay.

So why didn't I just say that in the first place? Why did I write this stupid book telling you how to fix your life if it was never going to fix your life?

Why not just tell you to let everything be okay and be done with it?

No reason at all other than, as I've already said, *it's not easy, it's not appealing,* and you almost certainly *wouldn't believe it.*

I mean, I ask you: If I had just said from the outset, *let it all be okay.* Would you have been happy with that advice? Would you have known 'how' to do it?

This warrants a book of its own or even several books. The difficulty of constantly or repeatedly *letting everything be okay* is the one reason I created my *Academy of Magic*—to provide a constant reminder of this truth.

Here's the thing, even when you've recognised the power of *letting everything be okay*, techniques like *The Ultimate Technique* will continue to be helpful and necessary...

...until they're not.

And I'll just explain this paradox as best I can.

At the beginning of the book, I mentioned a tightrope that we must walk—between trying to make things happen on the one hand, and letting everything be okay on the other. Keeping one foot in the everyday world of things and stuff and one foot in the magical realm.

But there's a funny thing about this tightrope that I've only realised fairly recently:

As we walk further along this path, the tightrope becomes more difficult to see and the two sides that seemed so paradoxical—the conflict between changing things while letting them be okay—becomes more indistinct. Eventually, the two sides seem almost to fuzz over... until they blur into one. And then you realise. There never was a path, nor a conflict, nor a paradox. The tightrope has disappeared. The paradox has disappeared. And in its place is just *this*. How things are. Everything, every possibility existing here in potential for you to enjoy, to create, to experience. And rather than decisions about what to do or attempts to 'let everything be okay', there is just you taking action in the moment without the slightest bit of resistance or confusion.

Everything simply *is* okay, profoundly okay.

The tightrope is now long gone, and you are dancing with life. *And the whole world suddenly opens up before you, complete wisdom, complete okayness, complete perfection—all for you.*

Everything you have ever wanted.

But here's the thing: you can't *make* the tightrope disappear. You can't decide to place yourself in this perfect now-world. You can't just choose to plunge wholeheartedly into the magical realm and stay there.

Understanding and knowledge of the perfection of this world is all there for the taking, but I cannot give it to you, nor can you think your way there. It *only* comes from your own direct experience.

The knowledge only comes from the doing.

Now, I've written this book because when it came to my own 'path', my own learning, my own journey, I had to do and do and do. I had to make things and create things. I had to learn to manipulate my reality in every possible way. I had to master 'manifesting'. I had to learn how to use magic to create stuff, effect change and get my life just right (or just as I thought it should be).

I needed to make stuff happen, I needed the law of attraction and manifesting. I needed to get my world 'right', *just so* that I could come to realise that I never needed to do that in the first place. I couldn't get to the end of the pathless path without taking the steps.

And so, I offer you this final, 'ultimate' *ultimate* technique. Make your world perfect so that you can come to see that it was already perfect all along.

I offer you this technique as a rung on a ladder you will eventually kick away, but only once you have used it to climb up.

To master *The Ultimate Technique*, we simply:

Decide something is so.

Tell a new story that fits it.

See, hear, sense, and feel the new story.

Take actions that support the new story.

Cast all evidence to the contrary as fluke or otherwise to be explained away.

And keep going until we believe it.

Or, we could just let everything, every tiny thing be profoundly okay in this moment and surrender completely to the flow of life.

Best of all, we do *both*!

We use all our capacities and sensibilities to create a 'better' world, while letting this one be absolutely and completely fine as it is. We recognise the perfection of this moment, while also moving in the direction of better things. We keep a foot in both worlds, until they reveal themselves to be one. We walk along the tightrope until it disappears. We climb that ladder until we can kick it away. We climb a ladder we will eventually see as completely nonsensical. We climb a ladder of illusion that points to truth.

And at some point, we will come to the end of playing around in, describing, or manipulating this illusion. We will, in a sense, step outside it, kick away the ladder, and move on to the next stage.

But until that stage, use *The Ultimate Technique*. Keep a foot in both worlds. Walk the tightrope until it starts to disappear. Make all the things and get all the stuff and enjoy every single footstep on this incredible journey.

About Genevieve

Genevieve Davis (real name, Sasha Stephens) is the author of over twenty books, including five on the subject of using magic to create a better life.

Becoming Magic
Doing Magic
Advanced Magic
Becoming Rich
Magic Words and How to Use Them

Her memoir, *Becoming Genevieve,* details the spiritual journey that led her to discover magic. Genevieve lives in the south of England with her partner, Mike and their two cats. For all inquiries, do visit the main website.

www.becomingmagic.com

Made in United States
Troutdale, OR
11/05/2023

14313212R00094